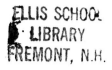
# OSCEOLA

## *Seminole Warrior*

*by Joanne Oppenheim*
*illustrated by Bill Ternay*

**Troll Associates**

Troll Associates, Mahwah, N.J.

Library of Congress Catalog Card Number: 78-60116
ISBN 0-89375-158-8

# OSCEOLA
## *Seminole Warrior*

Bright flames filled the dark night sky over the small Creek village.

"Come, Little Owl," said the boy's mother. "There is nothing left for us here."

He knew it was true. For two days the old men, women, and children had been hiding in the woods. He had heard the loud guns and war cries. His village was in flames. Many of the braves had been killed.

"One day I will fight the white men who did this," the boy promised himself. His heart was full of anger as he turned away.

For all of his ten summers, Little Owl had lived by the Tallapoosa River in Georgia. The people in his village had always lived in one place, raising cattle, hunting, and farming the land.

His life had been happy. Like other Creek boys, he longed for the day when he would become a warrior and earn his grown-up name.

But trouble had come to the Indians of the South. The Americans and the English had gone to war in 1812. Some of the Creeks had sided with the Americans. They were called the White Stick Creeks. The Red Sticks, Little Owl's people, remained friendly with the British.

Now General Andrew Jackson was marching with Bluecoats through Alabama and Georgia, burning villages and punishing Indians who were friends of the English.

7

General Jackson gave the White Sticks guns. The Red Sticks had only bows and arrows. They could not win.

It was not long before their homes, their cattle, and their corn had been destroyed.

Traveling from one hiding place to the next, Little Owl's people moved southward, leaving the land of their fathers behind them. They hoped to find English soldiers. If they had guns, perhaps they could win their lands back again.

But the war ended. The English were defeated . . . and could not help them.

Now the Red Sticks had no home. They were weary and hungry; they had lost everything.

Their only hope was to make a new home in the Spanish-owned land of Florida.

During the last century, many other Creek Indians also had been forced to run away from their hunting grounds in Alabama and Georgia. They had formed a large tribe in Florida called the Seminoles, which means *runaways*.

When the ragged band of Red Sticks reached northern Florida, the friendly Seminoles welcomed them. They helped their Creek brothers build new houses and prepare new fields. Then the women and children planted corn, beans, and squash.

In the forests, they found good hunting. From the lakes they took many fish.

Little Owl's mother sang happy songs again. They began to feel safe in their new home.

But the peace in northern Florida did not last. Night after night, Little Owl was awakened by the sound of distant gunfire.

Many Black slaves were fleeing Southern plantations to find safety and freedom with the friendly Florida tribes.

Men on horseback, paid to recapture the runaway slaves, rode into Indian villages. They brought violence and destruction with them. They stole cattle, and sometimes set fire to the Indians' houses and fields.

Late one night, Little Owl stood watch over the cattle and ponies. He heard a sound. For a moment, he thought it was thunder. Then, suddenly, the air was filled with the sound of bugles and guns! It was the Bluecoats again!

Little Owl was thrown to the ground as the cattle broke loose. Within minutes, the village was ablaze. Many braves lay wounded or dead.

Once again, the Red Sticks were left without a home.

"We will go farther south," said the leaders, "far from the borders of Georgia and Alabama."

After many weary weeks, they came to Tampa Bay. Here they felt they would be safe. The waters and swampy grasslands were rich with food. The crops would be good. It was warm in this land, even when the winter moons came.

Their Seminole neighbors were kind. They showed the Creeks how to build cool houses. They put long poles into the ground and covered the walls and roofs with green palmetto leaves. They called these houses *chickees*.

As the seasons passed, Owl learned to move silently in the forest. He went to hunt for deer, bear, and wild turkey.

The Seminoles showed his people how to paddle quickly and quietly through the twists and turns of the wild swamps. Sometimes they would bring home a special treat for the village—alligator tails and rattlesnake meat made fine feasting!

Gradually, the people of the Red Sticks began to think of themselves as Seminoles.

By the time Owl had reached his fifteenth summer, he had become known as the fastest runner, strongest wrestler, and finest hunter among the young men of the tribe. And he had proved himself to be a brave and fearless warrior.

Now, at last, he was ready to receive the name of his manhood.

For the ceremony, he dressed in his blue breechcloth. He painted his body blue. This was a sacred day, the most important day of his life.

The medicine men gave each new warrior a gourd full of a bitter black drink that they believed would bring great courage and power.

The young men sat still and silent. All day they ate nothing, but prayed to the Great Spirit until sunset.

Owl had dreamed of this day. He was no longer a boy. He prayed that the Great Spirit would make him a mighty warrior, strong and unafraid.

From that day on, he was known as Osceola.

18

Now Osceola was old enough to sit at the council fires. He listened as the Chiefs spoke of more trouble with the soldiers from the north.

20

General Andrew Jackson and 3,000 men were marching through Florida. Many Indians were still angry about the lands that had been taken from them in Georgia and Alabama. The government wanted to make sure there would be no more uprisings.

For several years there were uneasy times. The Indians learned that the government in Washington wanted more land.

The Chiefs were bitter and fearful. They had lost their homes many times before.

In 1823, the Americans sent word to the Chiefs: they must come to a meeting by the waters of Moultrie Creek.

As the council fires burned, Osceola remembered the flames of his boyhood village.

The Seminoles chose Chief Neamathla to lead them to Moultrie Creek. They followed a warrior who carried a white flag as a sign of peace.

The government agent told the Seminoles that they must move from their villages on the east and west coasts of Florida. For their land, they would be paid each year for twenty years.

"No!" Neamathla cried out.

"If you do not go," the agent said, "there will be much bloodshed."

22

For two days the Chiefs spoke together. Osceola and the other young men were ready to fight.

"There are many Bluecoats," said Neamathla. "If we do not agree, they will take what we have and give us nothing."

So the Treaty of Moultrie Creek was signed in 1823. The Seminole people agreed to move to a reservation in the central part of Florida.

Osceola was chosen to help the Bluecoats mark the boundary lines of the reservation.

His anger grew stronger as he saw that his people would be fenced in on useless land. Digging down in the soil, he found white sand. Corn would not grow here.

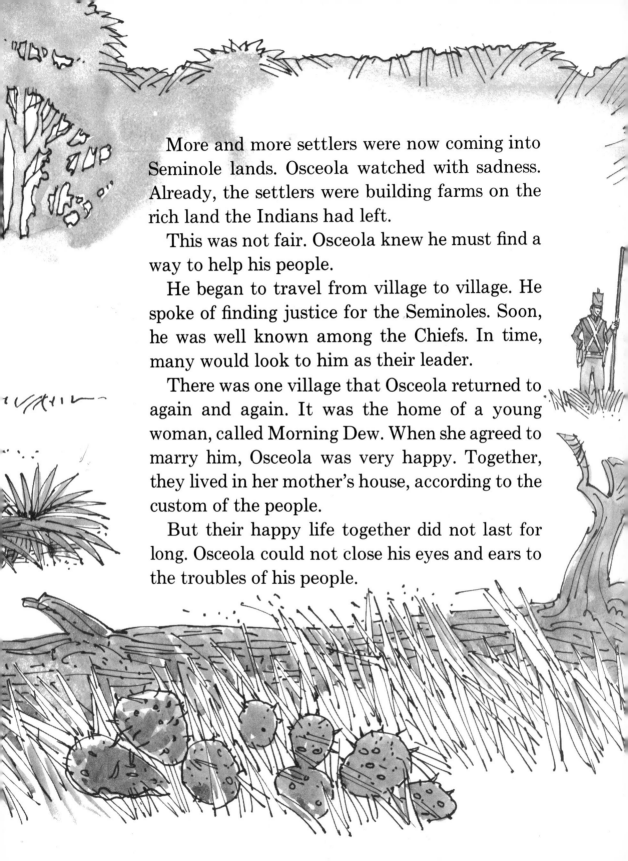

More and more settlers were now coming into Seminole lands. Osceola watched with sadness. Already, the settlers were building farms on the rich land the Indians had left.

This was not fair. Osceola knew he must find a way to help his people.

He began to travel from village to village. He spoke of finding justice for the Seminoles. Soon, he was well known among the Chiefs. In time, many would look to him as their leader.

There was one village that Osceola returned to again and again. It was the home of a young woman, called Morning Dew. When she agreed to marry him, Osceola was very happy. Together, they lived in her mother's house, according to the custom of the people.

But their happy life together did not last for long. Osceola could not close his eyes and ears to the troubles of his people.

Driven by hunger, Seminole warriors made raids on the settlers' cattle. They stole corn for their children. In their anger, the Indians burned barns and houses.

Osceola's worst fears were coming true.

"The boundary lines must be moved," he said, "or we will all starve."

Their troubles became worse. In 1829, General Jackson became president of the United States. In May of 1830, he passed a law that changed the lives of all American Indians. This law said that all tribes must move west of the Mississippi River.

In 1832, at Payne's Landing, there was another meeting. The government agent wanted the Seminoles to sign another treaty.

"This paper does not say you must move," said the agent. "It only says you will send some of your leaders to look at the land in the West. If they see that the land is good, in three years' time you will go in peace."

Osceola stood with his arms folded on his chest. He did not trust these words. His heart was heavy as the Chiefs signed the paper, one by one.

When the Chiefs returned from the land beyond the Great River, they shook their heads. How could they take their people so far from their own lands? Many feared that this would be the end of their Nation.

Osceola was angry. He spoke to the Chiefs.

"They have tricked us for the last time. We will not give up our land."

The Chiefs nodded in agreement.

"Their paper says we have three years to get ready. We must use the time well. We must buy gunpowder and lead. We must store food and guns.

"We do not want war, but we are not afraid to fight!"

As time passed, the anger between the Indians and the government grew stronger. Osceola felt that it was not long before there would be war again.

In 1835, a letter came from President Jackson. He told the Seminole leaders that he would not wait any longer. Now they must sign a treaty giving up their lands for good.

28

If the Indians did not move at once, a great army of Bluecoats would come to destroy them!

The government agent called the names of the Chiefs one at a time. Some stood firmly, but a few came forward and made their marks on the paper.

29

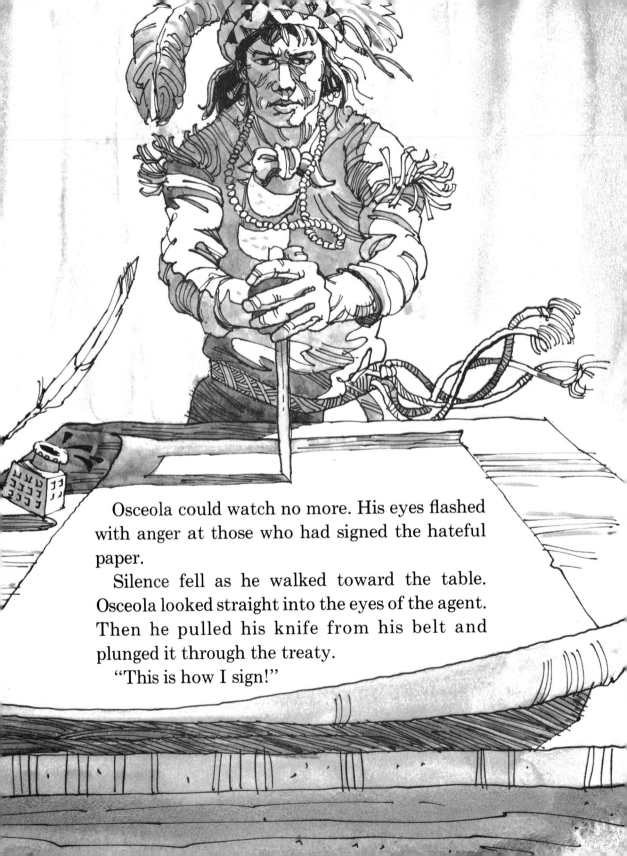

Osceola could watch no more. His eyes flashed with anger at those who had signed the hateful paper.

Silence fell as he walked toward the table. Osceola looked straight into the eyes of the agent. Then he pulled his knife from his belt and plunged it through the treaty.

"This is how I sign!"

By a blazing council fire, the Seminoles chanted a song of war. Now they must choose a strong and mighty War Chief to lead them.

Osceola was well known to the Chiefs and admired by the young warriors.

"Osceola!" they cheered. "Osceola will be our leader!"

Osceola was both proud and sad. He knew the horror war would bring. His people had suffered hunger and sickness. Soon many soldiers would come. They too would suffer.

"My people, we have asked only to live in peace on our land. The Bluecoats want no peace. They want only our land. We must stand together and fight. We will never leave the land!"

"Yo-ho-e-hee!"

The Seminole war cry echoed all over Florida!

Small bands of warriors made raids on the settlers. They burned their houses, barns, and fields.

They burned bridges along the roadways.

Soon no wagon train of supplies was safe from surprise attack.

No matter how they tried, the soldiers could not catch the Seminoles.

Osceola and his people knew the ways of the swamp. They knew the Bluecoats would be lost and frightened in the wild, marshy places where snakes and alligators could strike.

On islands in the green water, the Seminoles built small villages. Osceola's spies watched the soldiers. Their wagons moved slowly, but a brave could bring news quickly.

Hidden in the swamp, Osceola could pick his own time and place to attack.

In February of 1836, long lines of Bluecoats marched down the Withlacoochee River. They hoped to defeat the Seminoles once and for all. But they marched in the open. Osceola and the Indians hid and waited for the right moment.

"Yo-ho-e-hee!" Osceola cried out, as his warriors opened fire.

36

For eight days the battle raged. The Bluecoats suffered great losses.

But when more Bluecoats came to the rescue, Osceola and his men disappeared once again into the swamps.

Month after month, more soldiers came, but they could not break the spirit of Osceola and his warriors. The fighting continued, and one general after another left Florida in defeat.

By the summer of 1836, Osceola held most of western Florida.

But he felt no joy. His people were growing tired of war. They no longer had homes. Their families were gone.

The war had brought great pain and suffering to the Seminoles. Now, a terrible sickness, malaria, was killing Seminoles and settlers alike.

Osceola, himself, was weak and sick with fever.

Then, in the summer of 1837, General Thomas Jesup came with 5,000 fresh troops.

Jesup wanted one thing above all else. He wanted to capture the mighty War Chief Osceola!

By now, Osceola was very sick.

He decided it was time to talk peace with the Americans.

In October, 1837, Osceola made camp with a small band of his warriors, about seven miles from the General's fort at St. Augustine.

"Even though we have won great victories, we can never win the war against the Americans," he told his men.

"I will go to General Jesup under a flag of truce."

So it was that Osceola, weary and ill, went to General Jesup carrying a white flag.

"Have you come to surrender?" General Jesup asked.

Osceola stood tall and proud.

"I come to talk of peace. I will never surrender!"

Jesup had long planned for this moment.

"Take him!" he shouted.

Osceola was surrounded. His white flag was thrown to the ground. He stood silent as the soldiers put chains on his hands and feet.

Many soldiers turned away from the General. He had not acted with honor.

"Without Osceola, the war will soon be over!"

General Jesup was wrong about the Seminoles. They were so angry at Osceola's capture that for five more years they continued to fight!

But for Osceola, the war had ended. He was sent to prison—first in St. Augustine, later in Charleston, South Carolina.

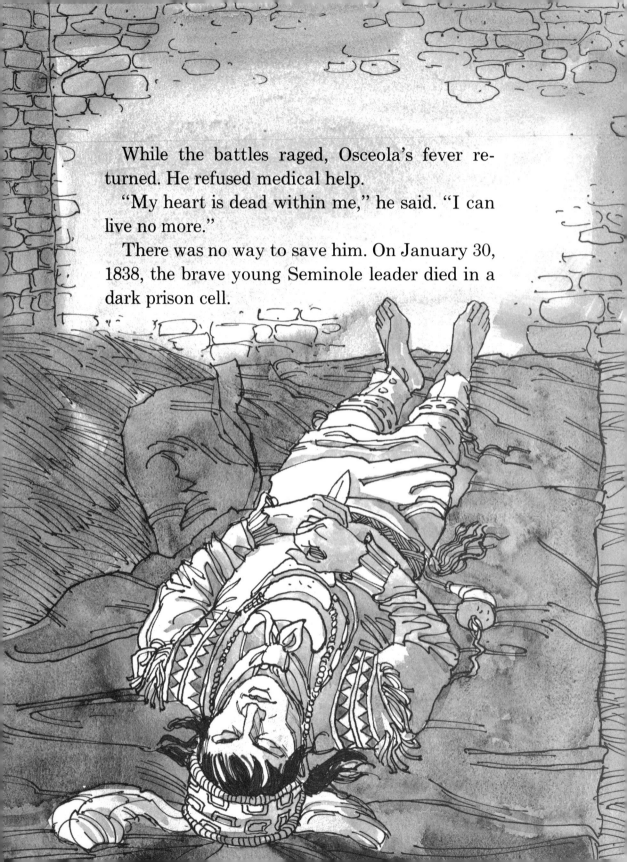

While the battles raged, Osceola's fever returned. He refused medical help.

"My heart is dead within me," he said. "I can live no more."

There was no way to save him. On January 30, 1838, the brave young Seminole leader died in a dark prison cell.

In time, the war ended. Many Seminole Indians had died. Many more were sent west of the
Mississippi to live.

But some never left Florida. Remembering Osceola's belief that Florida belonged to the Seminoles, they stayed hidden in the deep swamps.

Today their children and their children's children still live in the land Osceola loved.